W9-CAI-243

GREAT
AMERICAN PRESIDENTS

RONALD
REAGAN

GREAT
AMERICAN PRESIDENTS

_____ GREAT _____
AMERICAN PRESIDENTS

RONALD
REAGAN

BALDWIN PUBLIC LIBRARY

HEATHER LEHR WAGNER

FOREWORD BY
WALTER CRONKITE

CHELSEA HOUSE
PUBLISHERS
A Haights Cross Communications Company

Philadelphia

CHELSEA HOUSE PUBLISHERS

VP, NEW PRODUCT DEVELOPMENT Sally Cheney
DIRECTOR OF PRODUCTION Kim Shinners
CREATIVE MANAGER Takeshi Takahashi
MANUFACTURING MANAGER Diann Grasse

STAFF FOR RONALD REAGAN

ASSISTANT EDITOR Kate Sullivan
PRODUCTION ASSISTANT Megan Emery
ASSISTANT PHOTO EDITOR Noelle Nardone
SERIES DESIGNER Keith Trego
COVER DESIGNER Keith Trego
LAYOUT 21st Century Publishing and Communications, Inc.

A Haights Cross Communications ✦ Company

www.chelseahouse.com

First Printing

1 3 5 7 9 8 6 4 2

Library of Congress Cataloging-in-Publication Data

Wagner, Heather Lehr.
  Ronald Reagan / by Heather Lehr Wagner.
    p. cm.—(Great American presidents)
Includes bibliographical references and index.
Contents: The price of peace—"Dutch" Reagan—All-American in Hollywood—
From California governor to U.S. President—The White House: 1981-1984—The
White House: 1985-1988—The Reagan revolution.
  ISBN 0-7910-7604-0 (hardcover)   0-7910-7779-9 (PB)
  1. Reagan, Ronald—Juvenile literature. 2. Presidents—United States—Biography—
Juvenile literature. [1. Reagan, Ronald. 2. Presidents.] I. Title. II. Series. III. Series: Great
American presidents
E877.W33 2003
973.927'092—dc21
                                                                            2003007317

TABLE OF CONTENTS

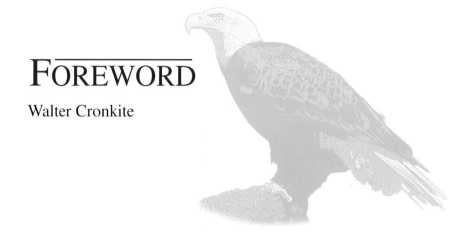

FOREWORD

Walter Cronkite

A candle can defy the darkness. It need not have the power of a great searchlight to be a welcome break from the gloom of night. So it goes in the assessment of leadership. He who lights the candle may not have the skill or imagination to turn the light that flickers for a moment into a perpetual glow, but history will assign credit to the degree it is due.

Some of our great American presidents may have had a single moment that bridged the chasm between the ordinary and the exceptional. Others may have assured their lofty place in our history through the sum total of their accomplishments.

When asked who were our greatest presidents, we cannot fail to open our list with the Founding Fathers who put together this nation and nursed it through the difficult years of its infancy. George Washington, John Adams, Thomas Jefferson, and James Madison took the high principles of the revolution against British tyranny and turned the concept of democracy into a nation that became the beacon of hope to oppressed peoples around the globe.

Almost invariably we add to that list our wartime presidents—Abraham Lincoln, perhaps Woodrow Wilson, and certainly Franklin Delano Roosevelt.

Nonetheless there is a thread of irony that runs through the inclusion of the names of those wartime presidents: In many aspects their leadership was enhanced by the fact that, without objection from the people, they assumed extraordinary powers to pursue victory over the nation's enemies (or, in the case of Lincoln, the Southern states).

The complexities of the democratic procedures by which the United States Constitution deliberately tried to withhold unchecked power from the presidency encumbered the presidents who needed their hands freed of the entangling bureaucracy that is the federal government.

Much of our history is written far after the events themselves took place. History may be amended by a much later generation seeking a precedent to justify an action considered necessary at the latter time. The history, in a sense, becomes what later generations interpret it to be.

President Jefferson in 1803 negotiated the purchase of vast lands in the south and west of North America from the French. The deal became knows as the Louisiana Purchase. A century and a half later, to justify seizing the nation's steel mills that were being shut down by a labor strike, President Truman cited the Louisiana Purchase as a case when the president in a major matter ignored Congress and acted almost solely on his own authority.

The case went to the Supreme Court, which overturned Truman six to three. The chief justice, Fred Vinson, was one of the three justices who supported the president. Many historians, however, agreed with the court's majority, pointing out that Jefferson scarcely acted alone: Members of Congress were in the forefront of the agitation to consummate the Louisiana Purchase and Congress voted to fund it.

With more than two centuries of history and precedent now behind us, the Constitution is still found to be flexible when honest and sincere individuals support their own causes with quite different readings of it. These are the questions that end up for interpretation by the Supreme Court.

As late as the early years of the twenty-first century, perhaps the most fateful decision any president ever can make—to commit the nation to war—was again debated and precedent ignored. The Constitution says that only the Congress has the authority to declare war. Yet the Congress, with the objection of few members, ignored this Constitutional provision and voted to give President George W. Bush the right to take the United States to war whenever and under whatever conditions he decided.

Thus a president's place in history may well be determined by how much power he seizes or is granted in re-interpreting and circumventing the remarkable document that is the Constitution. Although the Founding Fathers thought they had spelled out the president's authority in their clear division of powers between the branches of the executive, the legislative and the judiciary, their wisdom has been challenged frequently by ensuing generations. The need and the demand for change is dictated by the march of events, the vast alterations in society, the global condition beyond our influence, and the progress of technology far beyond the imaginations of any of the generations which preceded them.

The extent to which the powers of the presidency will be enhanced and utilized by the chief executives to come in large degree will depend, as they have throughout our history, on the character of the presidents themselves. The limitations on those powers, in turn, will depend on the strength and will of those other two legs of the three-legged stool of American government—the legislative and the judiciary.

And as long as this nation remains a democracy, the final say will rest with an educated electorate in perpetual exercise of its constitutional rights to free speech and a free and alert press.

1

THE PRICE
OF PEACE

ON NOVEMBER 19, 1985, Ronald Wilson Reagan, the 40th president of the United States, woke early and gazed out the window of the villa that was his temporary home. The November landscape was gray despite the morning light. Mist rose over the lake, and the sky was heavy with dark clouds. It was an ominous view for the president as he prepared for one of the most important meetings of his presidency. He had come to Geneva, Switzerland, to meet with Mikhail Gorbachev, the eighth leader of the Soviet Union.

Relations with the Soviet Union had become increasingly tense since Reagan's election in 1980. He had made no secret of his

This Intercontinental Ballistic Missile (ICBM) is paraded through Moscow's Red Square on May 9, 1965, in a display of the Soviet Union's military strength. Reagan would make nuclear disarmament one of the main goals of his presidency.

dislike of the Communist political system that governed the Soviet Union. In one famous speech in 1983, he had even referred to it as an "evil empire."

At the time of the meeting, the United States and the Soviet Union were the two most powerful nations in the world. Both countries covered vast stretches of territory, the United States in North America and the Soviet Union in Asia and Eastern Europe. Also, both countries possessed nuclear weapons.

Both of these countries and their leaders had made it clear that they would not accept second place in the competition for international influence. Under Reagan, the United States had built up its defense capabilities after years of cutbacks. Reagan believed that the only way to demonstrate the United States' seriousness in negotiation was to ensure that it operated from a position of strength. Reagan often used the phrase "peace through strength" to explain the reason for increased military spending.

As hostilities between the countries increased, and as the United States developed new missile technology and the Soviet Union occupied Afghanistan and began establishing a presence in Nicaragua, the war of words took on a more threatening tone.

The two leaders who came to Geneva could be considered the world's two most powerful men. The nuclear weapons they controlled could destroy each other's people and affect the entire world. The citizens of both countries feared the other's nuclear power. The threat was clear; the need for negotiation was even more clear.

President Reagan had come to Geneva to demonstrate that he wanted peace, not "peace at any cost"—he had no intention of giving in or giving up what he felt was critical for America's security—but he wanted to express to the Soviets (and to Americans) his belief that the best path for peace lay in a world free of nuclear weapons.

Reagan believed in the value of personal communication: Much of his political success came from his ability to connect with people. He was called "The Great Communicator" because of his skill as a politician.

Reagan's efforts to establish a personal connection

with the leader of the Soviet Union were made more difficult by the fact that there had been so many Soviet leaders since he became president. When Reagan was elected in 1980, the Soviet Union was led by Leonid Brezhnev, who had negotiated a policy of "détente" (relaxation of international tension) in the 1970s with then-president Richard Nixon. Reagan did not believe that the policy of détente was working and felt that the Soviet Union would respond better to a clear demonstration of strength.

Reagan felt that the policy of previous presidents—to speak politely about the Soviet Union and its leadership in public and make diplomatic efforts in private—had done little to benefit the United States. When he became president, he made it clear that a new age in Soviet–American relations, an age that would better benefit the United States, had begun. The new relationship was characterized by sharply critical words in public and no private contact at all. The Soviets responded in similar fashion.

> "Let us be aware that while they [the Soviet leaders] preach the supremacy of the state, declare its omnipotence over individual man, and predict its eventual domination of all peoples on the earth, they are the focus of evil in the modern world."
>
> — President Reagan's remarks at the Annual Convention of the National Association of Evangelicals, Orlando, Florida, on March 8, 1983

Reagan would later claim that his strategy was based on the goal of achieving peace by demonstrating that the United States sought peace not because it was needed but because it was wanted. He believed that arms control, and ultimately the elimination of nuclear weapons, could happen only if the United States entered negotiations in a position of military superiority. Reagan felt that previous arms control talks between the United States and the Soviet Union had left the impression that the United States was a weaker partner. He had no intention of allowing this to continue.

Reagan authorized the deployment of the controversial MX Peacekeeper long-range intercontinental ballistic missile (ICBM) in underground silos in Wyoming. The system was designed to prevent a first strike from the Soviets by ensuring that the U.S. forces that would strike back could survive an attack from Soviet ICBMs. This was done at a time when Soviet leadership was changing. Brezhnev had died on November 11, 1982. The new leader was a man named Yuri Andropov, the former head of the KGB, the Soviet Union's secret police.

Little progress was made in arms control negotiations under Andropov. Debates raged over the United States' efforts to position intermediate-range NATO (North Atlantic Treaty Organisation, an alliance of 19 North American and European countries) missiles in Western Europe, scheduled for the end of 1983. The chill increased on August 31, 1983, when Soviet air defense forces in the Far East shot down a Korean Air Lines passenger jet that had strayed into Soviet air space. All 269 passengers on board, including a U.S. congressman and 60 other Americans, died.

Reagan wasted no time in criticizing the incident in

This Peacekeeper missile is tested at the Vandenberg Air Force Base in southern California on March 7, 1986. President Reagan authorized the development of nuclear weapons, believing that the United States could better negotiate for peace from a position of strength.

the harshest possible terms. The Soviets responded by charging that the plane had been shot down because it was on a "spy mission" for the United States.

By early 1984, there was a new leader in the Soviet Union. Andropov had died after a long illness; Konstantin Chernenko was now in charge. It soon became clear that Chernenko was also ill and would probably not live long. Most foreign policy decisions, including the Soviet Union's boycott of the 1984 Olympics held in Los Angeles, were being made by another member of the leadership, Andrei Gromkyo.

Rumors of Chernenko's ill health proved to be true on March 11, 1985, when President Reagan learned that Chernenko had died and that his successor had been named. Mikhail Gorbachev was the new leader of the Soviet Union. Reagan was frustrated. "How am I supposed to get anyplace with the Russians," Reagan asked his wife Nancy, "if they keep dying on me?"

Gorbachev proved more willing to communicate than previous Soviet leaders had. He and Reagan exchanged detailed letters, confirming their agreement that a better relationship between the two superpowers needed to be established. Yet Gorbachev was no pushover. He expressed in strong terms his disapproval of the U.S. decision to deploy missiles in Western Europe, arguing that this action violated previously negotiated treaties. Ultimately, both sides agreed to a meeting in Geneva, Switzerland, a meeting at which the two leaders could share their concerns and, hopefully, begin to work toward a peaceful resolution of the ongoing conflict.

AN AMERICAN PRESIDENT

The historic meeting was scheduled to take place at Villa Fleur d'Eau, a 20-room castle overlooking Lake Geneva. Before the meeting, Reagan and his wife toured the grounds where the talks would be held, spotting a boathouse by the lake about one hundred yards from the castle. Reagan decided that the one-on-one communication he valued could best happen away from the formal negotiating table, apart from any support staff gathered to help with the discussions. Reagan asked members of his staff to prepare the boathouse by lighting a fire and setting up a more relaxed atmosphere.

Reagan arrived at the castle early on the morning of November 19. When Gorbachev arrived, Reagan hurried out to greet him. The media focused on the fact that Gorbachev wore a heavy coat and hat, whereas Reagan wore only his suit. It was popularly viewed as a "plus" for Reagan, giving the impression that he was more relaxed and comfortable, even in the chilly Geneva air.

Reagan focused more on the man than on what he was wearing and was surprised to discover that the new Soviet leader was warm and likeable. At a break in the conversations, Reagan suggested that they take a walk to the boathouse. Gorbachev quickly agreed.

The two leaders, accompanied only by their interpreters, sat across from each other by the blazing fire and

President Ronald Reagan greets the Soviet Union's leader Mikhail Gorbachev on November 19, 1985 at their first meeting in Geneva, Switzerland. The media was impressed by Reagan, who appeared comfortable in just a suit, while Gorbachev was bundled in a heavy coat and hat to keep warm in the cool Geneva weather.

began a conversation that would last an hour and a half. To help break the ice, Reagan focused not on their differences, but on what they had in common. He noted that they were two men from humble beginnings, born to poor families in small towns in the middle of their countries. They had risen to positions of such power that they were probably the only two men in the world who could bring about World War III, and yet they were also the only two men in the world who might be able to bring about world peace.

It was typical of Reagan's skill as a politician for him to focus on similarities and not differences in that early conversation. The differences between the men were numerous: At the time of the meeting, 74-year-old Reagan was the oldest American president to serve in office, and Gorbachev, at age 54, was young and healthy in comparison with previous Soviet leaders. Gorbachev had spent most of his life working for the Communist Party; Reagan had been a movie actor before entering politics. Reagan had been president for five years, and Gorbachev had led his nation for less than nine months.

The idea of two men from humble backgrounds deciding the fate of the world fit Reagan's idealistic vision. He had triumphed over a childhood marked by poverty and an alcoholic father. He held a deep belief in the essential goodness of people and a romantic view of America's role as an example for the rest of the world of what freedom and democracy could achieve.

Reagan did not consider himself a politician. He viewed himself as an ordinary citizen who, through chance and circumstance, had been given the opportunity to serve his country. He had come to Geneva determined to end the nuclear arms race and prevent a nuclear war.

Reagan understood the irony. He had become president while warning of the threat posed by the Soviets. Now he wanted to be the president who worked with the Soviet leader toward peace.

The meeting ended with both sides agreeing to meet again twice more—once in Washington, D.C., and once in Moscow. Their second meeting would instead take place in Reykjavik, Iceland, nearly a year later, and would end not in the smiling good humor of a fireside chat, but in bitter words and actions.

These summits showed an extraordinary evolution in the history of the United States and its relationship with the Soviet Union. They would also be the making of Ronald Reagan's legacy as president of the United States. The seeds first planted by Reagan would ultimately help bring about the end of the Soviet Union.

During his presidency, Reagan oversaw a dramatic transformation in the way Americans viewed themselves and their country. He described America as a "shining city on the hill," a beacon to other nations seeking freedom. He believed that one day, America would rise above all other countries to serve as a leader and role model.

Reagan's vision of a powerful America would become reality within his lifetime. Tragically, Alzheimer's disease—a disease that typically affects the elderly and causes lapses in memory and mental processes—would prevent him from fully appreciating his role in this transformation of global politics.

Ronald Reagan's life offers an astonishing portrait of the American dream—that is, the ability of anyone from even the most humble background to become anything he or she wanted, even president, and shape history through his or her words and actions. It is also a portrait of America at a turning point in its history, a period of time that would see the nation rise from the ashes of the Great Depression to a position of domination on the world stage.

2

"DUTCH" REAGAN

ON FEBRUARY 6, 1911, Jack and Nelle Reagan's second son Ronald was born. When Jack first saw the newborn, he said that the baby looked like a fat little Dutchman. As a young boy, Ronald asked to be called "Dutch," a name that he felt was more rugged than "Ronald."

Reagan's family was poor. They lived in Tampico, Illinois, where Ronald, his parents, and his two-year-old brother, Neil, were crammed into in a tiny one-bedroom apartment.

Reagan's mother, Nelle, was an evangelical Christian. She was known for her positive outlook and the belief that life had meaning and purpose and should be spent helping others. Many of her beliefs would become her sons', as well.

The young Ronald stands in front of his mother, Nelle, on the left in this Reagan family portrait from 1914. Ronald's older brother, Neil, and their father, Jack, stand to his right. Nelle and Jack instilled in their sons a sense of optimism and the belief that anything is possible.

Jack, Ronald's father, was always searching for something better from life and was willing to move from one place to another in search of greater opportunities. Jack was outspoken in his belief in the rights of working people. He also often spoke out against racial and religious prejudice, which was quite unusual for a man in the early twentieth century.

Jack struggled more with alcoholism than civil rights issues, and the family was often forced to move because he got and then lost jobs. They lived in tiny apartments and made do with very little. Ronald frequently struggled with being the new kid in school.

Ronald was often embarrassed by his father's drinking. As an adult, he would remember finding his father passed out in the snow on the front steps of their apartment building. He was only 11 years old at the time, and his mother had taken a job sewing for extra money and was not at home. Ronald managed to open the door, drag his father in, and put him to bed. As Reagan admitted later, what he had really wanted to do was simply step over his father, walk into the building, and close the door.

It was not an easy life for the young boy. His home was often filled with the sound of his parents fighting; at other times, the house would be tensely silent. Occasionally, Jack would disappear for several days, or the boys would be sent to stay with an aunt. There was never enough money, and the constant moving made it hard for Ronald to find friends.

COLLEGIATE ASPIRATIONS

When Ronald was nine years old, the family moved to Dixon, Illinois. Dixon was much larger than some of the other places the Reagan family had lived, but it still qualified as a small town. The town lay along the Rock River in northwestern Illinois. Ronald would look back on this time as one of the happiest of his life. To escape the tension in his family, he would hike along the cliffs and hills by the river. In winter, when the river froze, he would ice skate. In summer, he could swim or fish or even take overnight canoe trips.

Ronald also began to cherish a secret dream. His father had become part-owner of a shoe store in Dixon, and he assumed that one or both of his sons would join him in the business when they finished high school. Ronald found the work at the shoe store boring; he had bigger plans. He had read a series of books about college life that made it seem very glamorous. Ronald decided that he wanted to attend college and began looking for ways to earn money.

He worked part-time for a construction firm, earning 35 cents an hour. During the summer after his sophomore year in high school, he had a job working as a lifeguard. He spent seven summers working seven days a week, for 10 to 12 hours a day. During that time, he rescued 77 people from drowning, a statistic he quoted as one of his proudest accomplishments even after he became president. In fact, when Reagan began to suffer from Alzheimer's disease, the last job he would remember was lifeguarding along the Rock River.

EUREKA COLLEGE

One of the local heroes in Dixon was a boy named Garland Waggoner, a high school football star who had attended a small college about 110 miles away and had become a successful football player there. Reagan decided that if Eureka College was good enough for Garland Waggoner, it was the place for him.

Reagan had another reason for wanting to attend Eureka College: his girlfriend planned to go there, too. He was still hoping to save enough money for college when he drove her to campus to register for her freshman year. He took one look at the brick buildings and the green lawns and decided that he was not going to leave. He boldly found the college's president and its football coach and introduced himself, explaining that he was both a good football player and a great swimmer and could help win trophies for the school's teams.

> *"There are no such things as limits to growth, because there are no limits on the human capacity for intelligence, imagination, and wonder."*
>
> — Reagan, in his address to the University of South Carolina, Columbia, September 20, 1983

Reagan's communication skills—which would bring him great success later in life—must have been very persuasive even in his early years. The college not only gave him a scholarship that covered half of the tuition, but they also offered him a job that would cover the cost of food.

"Eureka" comes from a Greek word meaning "I have found it," and it seemed to Reagan in those first days on campus as if he had indeed found a special place where his dreams could begin to come true. The college was small, with no more than 250 students, and there were many opportunities to make friends and to get involved. It would also give Reagan his first experience in politics.

In 1928, during Reagan's freshman year of college, the country's economy was beginning to suffer, particularly in the Midwest. Within a year, the nation would experience the stock market crash and the Great Depression. At the same time, the college suffered a substantial drop in contributions, and the president decided that the only solution was to lay off some of the faculty members during the week that students went home for Thanksgiving.

The cuts would pose a problem to juniors and seniors, who might not be able to take the classes they needed to graduate. A student committee was organized, and Reagan was elected to serve as the freshman representative. When the cuts were formally announced, students and faculty quickly gathered in the campus chapel. Reagan stood up and began to speak, offering his thoughts on how the cutbacks would affect both students and the academic reputation of the college.

It was the first time that Reagan had given a formal speech in front of an audience. He concluded by calling for a student strike to protest the decision, and the audience responded with a roar of approval and thunderous applause. It was a defining moment for the young man.

ECONOMIC AND SOCIAL CHANGES

By Reagan's sophomore year, he had achieved another one of his goals: He made the starting lineup of the football team. For one away game, the team ended up in Dixon, Ronald's hometown, where they were supposed to spend the night. The coach told Ronald that he had to stay in a hotel with the rest of the team, so he went with the coach to the hotel to register. The hotel manager studied the team as they sat on the bus and told the coach that everybody could stay at the hotel except the team's two African-American players.

The coach was furious at the prejudice and said that they would all sleep on the bus that night, but Reagan suggested another solution. He told the coach to tell everyone that there weren't enough rooms in the hotel and that the team would have to split up. Reagan volunteered to take two of his teammates (the two African-American players) to stay at his house, where they were warmly welcomed by his mother.

The country was struggling with more than racial problems in those days; it was struggling with economic worries as well. In 1930, Reagan's father was forced to close his shoe store. Like many men, Jack left town and went in search of work—a search that seldom met with success. There were no jobs available, and radio broadcasts would regularly include messages advising people to not leave their homes because there were no work opportunities anywhere.

It was a frightening time for a young man. In 1932,

Reagan stands top and center in this autographed portrait of the Eureka College football team, taken in 1928. Reagan made the starting lineup of the college's football team during his sophomore year. He would later use his experience on the football field to achieve yet another goal—a career as a radio sports announcer.

the year that Reagan graduated from college, one out of every four adults in the country did not have a job. With such a grim picture facing him, Ronald struggled with the question, "What do I want to do with my life?"

Reagan loved acting. He had performed in many of the plays at Eureka. He was in love with the movies, too, but knew that he could not simply pack up and head off to New York or Hollywood. Instead, he set his sights closer, on Chicago, where much of the country's best radio broadcasting was done.

In the 1930s, radio programs played much the same

role that television does today. Radio offered a steady dose of entertainment—dramas, family programs, comedies, mysteries, and soap operas were all on the radio. Radio broadcasts of sporting events were also very popular. Because radio offered the opportunity to combine two of his greatest loves—performing and sports—he decided that he would become a radio sports announcer.

Reagan hitchhiked to Chicago, where he went to radio stations and received rejection after rejection. Finally, a woman at the NBC station in Chicago gave him some valuable advice. She told him that without experience he would not find work in a big-city market like Chicago. She advised him to find a radio job in a smaller town, get the experience he needed, and then come back. Discouraged, he hitchhiked back to Dixon.

After failing to find a job in his hometown, he decided to follow the advice of the woman at the radio station in Chicago. He borrowed his father's car and drove to Davenport, Iowa. He walked into the radio station WOC and asked to see the program director, explaining that he would take any job that was available.

The program director asked him if he knew anything about football. After learning that Reagan had played for eight years in high school and college, the director led him into a studio. "When the red light goes on," the director said, "I'll be in another room listening. Describe an imaginary football game to me and make me *see* it."

Reagan thought quickly and began to describe one

of the most exciting football games in which he'd played at Eureka College. Because he knew both the plays and the players, he was able to describe the game quickly and accurately, even adding a few touches to make the game more exciting. By the time Reagan finished, the station manager had reappeared with a smile on his face and offered Reagan a job broadcasting the Iowa–Minnesota Homecoming game for a salary of five dollars plus bus fare.

SPORTS ANNOUNCER FOR WHO

The job at WOC lasted only through the football season. Reagan returned home, where his father, a committed Democrat, had become involved in local politics. Jack was a strong believer in the policies of the newly elected president, Franklin Roosevelt, and persuaded his son to register as a Democrat and vote for Roosevelt in the next election.

Reagan was impressed by Roosevelt's ability to convey strength even though he had become president at a time of great economic crisis. He was impressed by the president's ability to give the people confidence during troubled times and by Roosevelt's reassuring radio broadcasts called "Fireside Chats."

Reagan soon was given another chance at radio. WOC offered him a job as a radio announcer, a job in which he would play music, read commercials, and introduce network and local broadcasts. Eventually, a new opportunity came to broadcast track meets from an affiliate station in Des Moines, Iowa, and Reagan was chosen.

Reagan became a sports announcer for WHO, a radio station based in Des Moines, Iowa, when he was only 22 years old. By broadcasting sporting events, Reagan made what was then a large salary—75 dollars a week— and developed the communication skills he would become known for in both his acting and political careers.

The Des Moines station, WHO, was one of the most powerful NBC radio stations in the country, and because of his good work on the track meets, Reagan was offered the position of sports announcer. It was his dream job, and he was great at it. At the age of 22, he was earning 75 dollars a week—a large salary during the Great Depression—and he was becoming famous through- out the Midwest. He covered football games, track meets, swimming competitions, and auto races.

Reagan's most notable radio broadcasts were of baseball games he never attended. A telegraph operator based wherever the Chicago Cubs or Chicago White Sox were playing would tap out a message in Morse code after each play and pitch. Another telegraph operator in Des Moines would decode the Morse message, translating it from dots and dashes into the few words that described the play and then hand it through a slot to Reagan, who would be seated at a microphone in the studio.

The messages would be very brief, but Reagan would take these few words and then describe the play as if he were seated in the stadium watching it. The description had to be done quickly because other radio stations were also broadcasting the games, some of them live. There would be air time between pitches and innings that Reagan would have to fill by talking about the players, the weather, and the field, none of which he could see.

Reagan came up with a plan that would help him escape the frigid Iowa cold. He offered to accompany the Chicago Cubs on their annual spring training camp in Catalina, California, telling the station that if it would pay his expenses, he would use his vacation time for the trip. The trip would provide him with behind-the-scenes knowledge of the team, an all-expense-paid trip to California, and something else: a chance to get a bit closer to his long-time dream of becoming an actor.

3

ALL-AMERICAN IN HOLLYWOOD

IN 1937, RONALD REAGAN was in California covering the Cubs'
spring training camp when he decided to visit a girl he knew who
was working in Hollywood. They had dinner, and during the meal
he told her about his dream of becoming a movie actor. She made
a call to an agent she knew, who agreed to meet him.

At the interview, the agent took a look at Reagan and quickly
placed a call to a casting director at Warner Brothers, who also
agreed to meet with Reagan. After the meeting, the casting
director offered him a screen test. Reagan was given a script to
memorize and returned a few days later to perform the lines.

Two days after Reagan returned to Des Moines, a cable arrived,

As a professional Hollywood actor, Ronald Reagan took many photographs for publicity and casting like this headshot. Around the time that this picture was taken in the late 1930s, Reagan was working steadily and dating the screen actress Jane Wyman, whom he would marry in 1940.

offering him a seven-year contract at 200 dollars a week. He quickly instructed his agent to sign before Warner Brothers withdrew the offer. Then he said his good-byes, packed up all of his belongings, and headed for California.

THE HOLLYWOOD ACTOR

Reagan had been warned that it might take months before he was cast in a movie, but he was working in his first movie within only a few days. In June 1937, Reagan began his acting career at Warner Brothers using his given name, Ronald Reagan, because movie executives thought "Dutch" Reagan did not sound like the name of a movie star. It was an amazing time for the 26-year-old radio announcer. Suddenly, he was surrounded by movie stars. People he had only seen on the screen of the movie theater were now working with him.

The movie was *Love Is in the Air*. Reagan played a radio announcer. Despite the fact that he was playing a role with which he was quite familiar, he was gripped by stage fright on his first morning. When the lights went on and the camera began to roll, however, his stage fright disappeared.

Three weeks later, the movie had finished filming. Before Reagan had time to worry about being unemployed, he was offered a role in a film entitled *Sergeant Murphy*. Other parts quickly followed. He was playing small roles—a cadet, a newspaperman, a teacher—but working steadily. Warner Brothers liked his work, renewed his contract, and gave him a raise. He was able to share his good fortune with his parents by moving them to California and buying them the first house they ever owned.

The part that would truly make Reagan a star was George Gipp ("the Gipper") in the movie *Knute Rockne,*

All American. The movie told the story of Knute Rockne, the coach at Notre Dame who helped revolutionize the game of football. Reagan's character was a football player who became Rockne's greatest star but died. In the movie, just before Gipp dies, he says to Rockne, "Some day when things are tough and the breaks are going against the boys, ask them to go in there and win one for the Gipper." When Reagan ran for president many years later, the media often referred to him as "the Gipper."

Reagan made *Knute Rockne, All American* in 1940 and that year brought him both professional and personal satisfaction. His portrayal of the emotional role moved him up to bigger roles in more important movies. He also married a young actress named Jane Wyman.

Reagan had met Wyman while filming his ninth movie, *Brother Rat,* in which she also had a part. They seemed well matched. Both were young, attractive, and ambitious with careers on the rise. One year after they married, their daughter Maureen was born. In 1945, they adopted a son, Michael.

WORLD WAR II AND COMMUNISM

World War II began when Reagan was 30 years old. Reagan was an officer in the United States Cavalry Reserves. Although his career was just taking off, he was called to active duty three months after the attack at Pearl Harbor. Because he had poor eyesight, he was not called to combat duty but instead was transferred to the air force

Reagan and his first wife Jane Wyman act in this scene from
Brother Rat in 1938. The young and attractive couple seemed
to be a perfect match. The couple would have two children, a
daughter named Maureen and an adopted son named Michael.

intelligence division of the army in Los Angeles, where he
worked making training films and documentaries.

He was in the armed services for four years. By the
time the war ended, new movie stars had become popular.

Reagan had hoped to take on bigger, more serious roles, but Warner Brothers continued to cast him in comedies.

In the years after the war, Reagan became increasingly involved with the labor issues affecting Hollywood. He was elected president of the Screen Actors Guild and in that position began to negotiate among different groups in Hollywood to resolve strikes or work disputes. He also became aware that the Communist Party was attempting to influence certain groups in Hollywood, including two organizations of which he was a member. He ultimately left both groups for this reason.

The United States and the Soviet Union had been allies during World War II, and the Communist Party had members throughout the country, including Hollywood. After World War II ended and the Cold War began, rumors began to spread of Communist attempts to influence the movie industry and, in this way, to influence all Americans through the movies they watched.

Reagan considered himself a Democrat and a liberal, but he was disappointed by the fact that so many liberals refused to speak out against Communist activities. He was called before the U.S. House of Representatives in its investigation of so-called "un-American activities." He refused to name anyone who might be a member of the Communist Party, but he spoke out against both Communism and anyone who might use "undemocratic means" to stamp it out. He also supported the Hollywood studios' plan to blacklist (refuse to hire) actors, writers, and others who refused to cooperate with the House investigation, explaining that an actor's reputation could affect the success of a film.

The shake-ups in Hollywood, the strikes, and the rumors deeply affected Reagan. The experience left him convinced that Communism posed a serious and lasting threat to what he believed America should represent.

As he became more active politically, his marriage was failing. Jane Wyman was enjoying a successful career as an actress and had won an Academy Award. When they married, both she and her husband were ambitious young actors with careers on the rise. Her career had taken off, but Reagan's had faded. Her focus still was on making movies; he was spending more and more time on political issues. They divorced in 1948. It was a sad, painful time for Reagan.

GENERAL ELECTRIC SPOKESMAN

Reagan made 22 movies after the war, but by the early 1950s, his career was fading. His life took a turn for the better when he was introduced to an actress named Nancy Davis. They quickly fell in love and were married on March 4, 1952. Davis soon gave up her acting career to focus on their family. Later in 1952, their daughter, Patti, was born. A son, Ronald Prescott Reagan, was born in 1958. The couple would appear in one movie together, *Hellcats of the Navy*.

By 1954, a new opportunity had begun to draw Reagan away from filmmaking. He had been approached to host a new television series sponsored by General Electric. In

After a painful divorce from Jane Wyman, Reagan met and fell in love with Nancy Davis, another Hollywood actress. After their wedding on March 4, 1952, Nancy quit acting to focus on their family, which would include a daughter, Patti, and a son, Ronald.

addition to hosting *General Electric Theater* on Sunday nights, Reagan would be responsible for giving speeches and making appearances at various General Electric plants. He jumped at the opportunity.

It was tremendous training for Reagan's political

future. At the time, General Electric had 135 plants in 38 states and a total of 250,000 employees. Reagan spent the next eight years traveling around the country, sometimes giving several speeches in a single day. He spoke before executives and employees, to large and small groups, developing his speaking skills.

He learned to listen, too. He heard certain common complaints from his audiences—about the size of the federal government and the rights of workers—many of which he shared.

This change in philosophy made it increasingly difficult for him to support the Democratic Party. In 1952, he cast his first vote for a Republican candidate, Dwight D. Eisenhower. He supported Eisenhower again when he ran for re-election. In 1960, he supported the campaign of Eisenhower's vice president, Richard Nixon, who was defeated by John F. Kennedy. In 1962, Reagan formally changed his party affiliation to Republican.

Reagan's speeches had always been heavily influenced by his political views, but with a popular Democratic president in the White House, his more conservative opinions seemed out of step with the rest of the country. Executives at General Electric asked him to confine his speeches to the company's products, but Reagan refused. As a result, General Electric did not renew his contract when the old one expired.

Reagan soon became more directly involved in politics. In 1964, he campaigned for Barry Goldwater, a Republican senator from Arizona who was running for president. Reagan was seen by some members of the Goldwater campaign as too conservative, by others as too controversial, and by others as simply a fading Hollywood star. All of that changed on October 27, 1964, when Ronald Reagan gave a speech on national television in support of Goldwater.

The speech would become known as "A Time for Choosing." The words were nothing radical or new for Reagan. They repeated many of the same thoughts he had shared in his General Electric appearances: the problems caused by government waste, the evils of Communism, and the importance of protecting individual freedoms.

Reagan's speech raised more than eight million dollars for the Republican Party, more money than any other political speech up to that time. Although Goldwater's campaign would fail, Reagan had positioned himself for political success.

> "You and I have the courage to say to our enemies, 'There is a price we will not pay.' There is a point beyond which they must not advance! . . . You and I have a rendezvous with destiny. We will preserve for our children this, the last best hope of man on earth, or we will sentence them to take the last step into a thousand years of darkness. If we fail, at least let our children and our children's children say of us we justified our brief moment here. We did all that could be done."
>
> — From the televised national speech Ronald Reagan gave on behalf of Senator Barry Goldwater on October 27, 1964

4

FROM CALIFORNIA GOVERNOR TO U.S. PRESIDENT

REPUBLICAN PARTY OFFICIALS had previously spoken with Ronald Reagan about becoming a candidate because of his strong political views. Reagan had never seriously entertained the idea, but after the overwhelming success of his Goldwater speech, he began to think that even at age 54, it was not too late for him to consider changing careers.

There were not many strong Republican candidates, and Reagan had received offers of support from many wealthy conservatives. He decided to test the waters in his home state, California, a place where being an actor was not necessarily a liability.

Reagan becomes the governor of California as he takes the oath of office from California State Supreme Court Justice Marshall F. McComb on January 2, 1967. Although Reagan was old at age 56 to be beginning a political career, he easily won public support from his over 30 years as a broadcaster and an actor.

He announced his run for governor on January 4, 1966. He was underestimated by the other Republican candidates, who thought of him as too conservative, and by the Democratic incumbent governor, Pat Brown, who was seeking his third term. Reagan was well known and liked from 30 years in movies and television; he was a strong speaker on television, on radio, and in person; and he had clear views and a firm vision. He won the Republican primary and began a campaign designed to reach out to independent and working-class Democrats.

The campaign proved successful. Reagan won the election by almost a million votes. On January 2, 1967, he was sworn in as the 33rd governor of California.

MEETING CALIFORNIA'S CHALLENGES

Reagan soon discovered significant problems with the state budget. According to the state's constitution, California's budget had to be balanced each year. Governor Brown had manipulated the numbers in 1966, leaving his successor with an unbalanced budget and a problem. Reagan's campaign had promised to cut taxes, but the only way to solve California's budget crisis was a tax increase.

Reagan faced other problems as well. His staff consisted largely of people who, like himself, were new to politics and to running a state government. Unpopular decisions, such as those to close mental hospitals, crack down on demonstrations at the University of California at Berkeley, and charge in-state tuition to students at public California universities, sparked criticism of the new governor.

Almost immediately after taking office, Reagan was forced to take a stand on abortion, a controversial issue. The Supreme Court decision known as *Roe v. Wade* did not occur until 1973, but in 1967, an act was introduced in the California state senate designed to permit doctors to perform abortions in certain cases. Women rallied around the petition, but leading Catholics and conservatives opposed it. In the end, Reagan signed the act. In later years, he would state that his decision to sign the bill came from his inexperience as governor and he would take a firm stand against abortion except in cases of rape, incest, or where the life of the mother was at risk.

Reagan learned from his early mistakes and was able to build alliances with California's Democratic state assembly and state senate. He demonstrated to these legislators his willingness to be practical in solving the state's problems and also showed that he kept his word. His experience negotiating with unions in Hollywood had given him the skills necessary to compromise without straying too far from certain basic goals.

By 1967, Reagan was under a new kind of pressure. Members of the California Republican Party wanted him to think about a new job: president of the United States.

Reagan tested the waters without formally announcing his candidacy. He traveled to traditionally conservative states in the South and West giving speeches. Even with Reagan's efforts, Richard Nixon quickly emerged as the leading Republican candidate, and it was Nixon who received the Republican Party nomination.

Reagan turned his attention back to California. He ran for a second term as governor, this time with a campaign focused on welfare reform. He easily won re-election in 1970.

ECONOMIC EFFORTS

Reagan kept his campaign promise of reforming the state's welfare system. Working closely with Democratic legislators, he helped to produce the California Welfare Reform Act of 1971, a plan designed to reduce welfare cheating and to provide more grants for the truly needy. The plan succeeded in reducing the number of people receiving welfare benefits, and the cooperative relationship developed between the governor and the state legislature helped pass other legislation, as well.

Reagan had become governor with a pledge to create a more cost-conscious government. He succeeded in some areas: he consistently worked to keep his budgets in line, he refused to increase state employment, and he urged more efficient use of resources within state offices. Still, the state budget more than doubled while he was governor.

Reagan resisted pressure to run for a third term. He was a popular governor, but by the time he left office in 1975, the Republican Party was suffering from the Watergate scandal and Richard Nixon's resignation. Reagan left Sacramento to return to his home in Pacific Palisades, but he was not thinking about retirement. He was thinking about another campaign: one for the presidency of the United States.

RACE FOR THE WHITE HOUSE

Reagan began his presidential campaign unofficially, perhaps preferring to analyze the situation before firmly committing to challenge then-President Gerald Ford for

Reagan formally announced his candidacy for president of the United States on November 20, 1975 with his wife Nancy by his side. Although Reagan had to compete fiercely with the current president, Gerald Ford, for the Republican nomination, he lost by only 117 votes.

the Republican nomination. He had been hired to give weekly radio talks and to write a weekly newspaper column, and he remained a popular speaker. All of these provided him with an opportunity to express his political views and build a base of popular support.

Reagan formally announced his candidacy on November 20, 1975. Most political experts felt that he had little chance of winning the nomination from Ford, and in the first primary, in New Hampshire, he did lose, although narrowly. Other defeats followed. Some Republicans urged him to give up, but Reagan was determined to make one last stand in the primary in North Carolina. In the days before this primary, Reagan shifted his focus to foreign policy issues, criticizing the Ford administration for its efforts to negotiate a return of the Panama Canal to the nation of Panama and for its unwillingness to match the military buildup going on in the Soviet Union.

The switch in focus helped Reagan win in North Carolina and in the next 20 primaries, the races were fiercely fought. By the time of the Republican National Convention, it was still not clear who the Republican nominee for president would be.

In the end, Reagan lost the nomination by only 117 delegate votes out of a possible 2,257. He thanked his supporters and got on a plane to California. He was 65 years old, but he wasn't thinking about retirement. He was thinking about the next presidential race.

THE 1980 CAMPAIGN

Ronald Reagan's next campaign for the presidency began immediately after he lost the Republican nomination. He set about building a network of supporters in the Republican Party by actively campaigning for Ford, traveling to 20 different states to speak on behalf of his former rival. He returned to his newspaper column and his radio broadcasts, promoting Republican candidates while sharing his ideas.

The strategy would begin to position Reagan as the leading Republican candidate for president in the 1980 election. By doing favors for other candidates and being visible after his 1976 campaign ended, he let the momentum build for the next four years.

Reagan studied Jimmy Carter, the man who ultimately won the presidency. He saw how Carter's policies were failing, how unemployment and inflation and interest rates were on the rise, and that the military was facing severe budget cuts. Reagan believed that these policies were wrong, and he did not hesitate to speak out against them.

There was one significant obstacle to Reagan's efforts to win the presidency in 1980: his age. If he won the election, he would be 70 years old shortly after inauguration, making him the oldest newly elected president in American history.

Reagan was determined not to let age prevent him from achieving this dream. On November 13, 1979, he again announced his candidacy. He was not the only man who dreamed of becoming the Republican candidate for president. Seven other Republicans had decided to enter the race. In the first challenge, the Iowa caucus, Reagan was defeated by George H.W. Bush. Bush subtly made Reagan's age an issue by jogging with reporters and members of his staff, demonstrating his energy. The tide turned in the New Hampshire primary. Reagan won the state and went on to win the nomination. He chose George H.W. Bush, clearly a strong politician, as his running mate.

Reagan did not hesitate to point out the Carter administration's weak points during the presidential campaign. In 1979, the Shah of Iran had fled the country and was replaced by fundamentalist ruler Ayatollah Khomeini. The crisis disrupted Iranian oil exports, causing oil prices to soar. Americans had to wait in lines at gas stations and were assigned specific days when they could buy gasoline. In November, Iranians seized 52 Americans at the American Embassy in Tehran and held them as hostages. On December 25, Soviet forces invaded Afghanistan. Americans were fighting high unemployment and inflation at home and an image of weakness overseas.

> "I believed . . . that America's greatest years were ahead of it, that we had to look at the things that had made it the greatest, richest, and most progressive country on earth in the first place, decide what had gone wrong, and then put it back on course."
>
> — Ronald Reagan on the belief on which his 1980 campaign for president was focused

Reagan's campaign was not flawless, but he remembered the optimism that Franklin Roosevelt demonstrated during the Depression. Reagan's cheerful, positive comments were in stark contrast to the more serious tones of the Carter message. Carter criticized Reagan as supporting war rather than peace and of weakening federal programs like Social Security by transferring control back to the individual states.

The Reagan campaign triumphed over Carter's with one simple question: "Are you better off now than you were four years ago?" For too many Americans, the answer was no.

5

THE
WHITE HOUSE:
1981–1984

RONALD REAGAN'S INAUGURATION on January 20, 1981, began with good omens. The weather was warmer than usual for a January in Washington, D.C., and as he took his place on the podium on the west front of the Capitol, the sun burst through the clouds, showering him with a burst of bright light. More importantly, on that day, following months of intense negotiations by both the Carter and Reagan teams, the 52 American hostages were finally released after 444 days in captivity in Iran.

Reagan's inaugural speech returned to one of his favorite themes: keeping government under control, thereby creating greater freedom for individual Americans. In the speech, he expressed his

The oldest candidate to be elected to the U.S. presidency, Ronald Reagan was sworn in as the 40th president of the United States on January 20, 1981. On that same day, negotiations from both Carter's and Reagan's teams would end successfully when 52 American hostages were released from Iran after being held captive for over a year.

belief that ordinary people freed from the burden of taxes and government interference would do great things and would work to make the country great, as well.

Reagan did not waste time. His transition team was in place before he was even elected, and he had begun the process of determining policy and deciding who would be offered jobs before his first day in the Oval Office.

Reagan believed that the immediate priority of his administration was addressing the country's economic crisis. He had entered office facing a dismal economic picture once before—when he first became governor of California—and he and his team immediately set to work to put new economic policies into place. On his first day in office, a freeze was ordered to stop additional federal employees from being hired. As he did in California, Reagan was quick to present his plan to the people, scheduling a television address in which he stated that the United States was facing serious economic problems and that "business-as-usual" would no longer work.

Reagan's belief was that tax reform would solve many of the country's economic problems. He proposed to reduce federal income tax rates for all taxpayers, believing that people paying less in taxes would have more money to spend on other things. Businesses would then be prompted to hire more workers, which would give more people income, enabling more people to pay taxes. This is a very simplified version of what came to be known as "supply-side economics" or "Reaganomics."

> "We have every right to dream heroic dreams. Those who say that we're in a time when there are no heroes, they just don't know where to look."
>
> — From Reagan's Inaugural Address, January 20, 1981

Reagan had been very specific about the goals of his administration during the campaign: reduce taxes, increase military spending, and cut domestic programs, except for Social Security. These became the focus of his early days in office.

THE ASSASSINATION ATTEMPT

On March 30, 1981, Reagan gave a luncheon speech to a large group of union representatives at the Washington, D.C., Hilton Hotel. He was hoping to gain support for his economic program.

He left the hotel through a side entrance, passing through a line of press photographers and television cameras. As he walked up to his limousine, he heard what sounded like firecrackers to his left. Just as he was asking what the noise was, the head of his Secret Service unit grabbed him by the waist and threw him into the back of the limousine. Reagan landed with his face on the armrest across the back seat, and the Secret Service agent then jumped in on top of him.

When the agent landed on him, Reagan felt an intense pain in his back and told the agent that he thought one of his ribs had broken. The agent ordered the driver to head for the White House, but as Reagan sat up, he coughed into his hand and saw that it was covered with blood. The agent saw the blood and ordered the driver to go to George Washington University Hospital.

Reagan continued to cough up blood and was

Jim Brady lies sprawled on the ground after being caught in the gunfire intended for President Reagan on March 30, 1981. Before the shooting had ended, John Hinckley Jr. had shot Reagan and three other men. The grace and wit Reagan displayed after the assassination attempt won him the love and support of the American public.

having trouble breathing. When they arrived at the hospital, he was able to walk into the emergency room but collapsed as soon as he was inside. The president had been shot, hit with a bullet designed to fly apart once inside its target. The bullet had lodged less than an inch from Reagan's heart.

When Nancy Reagan arrived at the White House, Reagan murmured to her, "Honey, I forgot to duck." Later, as he was being wheeled in for surgery, he jokingly told his doctor that he hoped he was a Republican. "Today, Mr. President, we're all Republicans," the doctor reassured him.

There were other victims that day: Jim Brady, Reagan's press secretary; Tim McCarthy, a Secret Service agent; and Tom Delehanty, a policeman. Although all of the men would survive the attack, Jim Brady, who was shot in the head, would be confined to a wheelchair for the rest of his life. The shooter was John Hinckley Jr., a troubled 25-year-old man who claimed that he had shot Reagan in order to impress actress Jodie Foster.

The assassination attempt, and Reagan's grace and wit after it, transformed his presidency. The public rallied around him, and former political opponents soon followed, with Republicans and Democrats cheering as he called for a tax cut in a speech delivered before Congress less than a month after he had been shot.

After the assassination attempt, Reagan wrote in his diary, "Whatever happens now I owe my life to God and will try to serve him in every way I can." Shortly after writing those words, Reagan began the process of what would become perhaps the greatest accomplishment of his presidency. On April 24, Reagan issued an order to lift the grain embargo (prohibition of sale) that President Carter had imposed against the Soviet Union when it invaded Afghanistan. On that same day, he sent a handwritten letter to Leonid Brezhnev, the Soviet Union's current leader, expressing his hope that by lifting the embargo he would begin a dialogue that could lead to peace. Neither action would result in an immediate change in the tensions between the United States and the Soviet Union, but Reagan would continue to attempt periodic contact until he finally connected with someone willing to talk back.

FIRST TERM CHALLENGES

Reagan faced an uphill battle in his first term. Although he was ultimately able to pass a modified version of the 30 percent cut in income tax he had initially wanted, Congress was unwilling to make the drastic budget cuts he had called for. A budget reduction calling for the elimination of Social Security's minimum benefit and a reduction in payments to workers who retired before age 65, as well as a reduction in disability payments, drew sharp criticism and was quickly voted down.

The next challenge to Reagan's leadership skills came in August 1981, when 13,000 air traffic controllers called for a strike. The air traffic controllers had demanded a substantial pay increase and refused the more modest increase Reagan had offered. Reagan made it clear that public safety was at stake and gave the air traffic controllers 48 hours to return to work. The union members refused, and Reagan announced that they would all be fired. It was a difficult decision, but it ultimately showed that he would keep his word no matter what and that he was serious about eliminating excessive spending.

Economic problems continued despite the changes the Reagan administration had enacted. For the first half of Reagan's first term, the economy struggled under a recession (a widespread slowing down in business activity).

In August 1981, 13,000 air traffic controllers went on strike for a substantial wage increase, despite the modest pay increase Reagan offered them. With public safety in jeopardy, Reagan kept his word and fired those strikers who did not return to work after the 48-hour time limit he had set.

Unemployment figures continued to rise; housing and automobile sales dropped.

It was a grim time for many Americans, but Reagan stuck to his plan and continued to project an image of confidence. He believed that the weak economy was the result of previous administrations' failures and that the country just needed time to work its way out of it. By April 1983, Reagan was proved correct. The recession had ended, and the economy would remain strong for the rest of his presidency.

Does this mean Reagan's economic plan was a success? Certainly the nation entered a six-year period of prosperity, with millions of new jobs created and an end to inflation. Reagan also accomplished his goal of cutting the income tax rate, reducing the top rate at which Americans were taxed from 70 percent of their income to 33 percent. Both unemployment and interest rates also dropped during Reagan's presidency.

THE REAGAN LEGACY

Reaganomics

Ronald Reagan's economic policy, which came to be known as "Reaganomics," was based on a theory known as supply-side economics. Supporters of this theory believe that government should promote economic growth by removing barriers to production and by cutting taxes and deregulating (removing restrictions on) industries in order to encourage people to work more and invest more.

President Reagan's economic goals were to reduce inflation, to speed up economic growth, to cut income taxes, to strengthen the military, to reduce the size of government, and to cut excessive regulation. These goals often came into conflict with each other, and Reagan's economic legacy showed this conflict. During his presidency, inflation was lowered, but budget deficits increased. Taxes were cut, but government spending increased. There were fewer economic regulations but more social regulations. While Reagan was in office, the country passed through a deep recession and began a lengthy recovery.

The result was a legacy of both accomplishments and disappointments. During his term in office, Reagan's economic plan helped Americans by reducing interest rates, reducing unemployment, and raising the average family income. However, the budget and trade deficits rose dramatically, leaving an expensive bill for Reagan's successor, George H.W. Bush, to decide how to pay.

There was a dark side to the economic picture, however. Reagan had hoped to create a more balanced budget, but the opposite happened. During Reagan's presidency, the national debt more than quadrupled, from 700 billion dollars to nearly 3 trillion dollars. The trade deficit also more than quadrupled. These budget problems were created in part because Reagan's administration drastically increased military spending without being able to make any major cuts in domestic spending. Also, the core of "supply-side economics" or "Reaganomics"—the belief that if the government cut taxes, people would have more money and spend it—failed to happen.

For most Americans, however, one simple fact was clear when they entered the voting booth in 1984 to vote for Ronald Reagan or his Democratic challenger, Walter Mondale, who had served as Jimmy Carter's vice president. When they asked themselves "Am I better off now than I was four years ago?" the answer was almost always a definite "yes." Reagan won in a landslide victory.

6

THE
WHITE HOUSE:
1985–1988

RONALD REAGAN'S SECOND term as president began with less of the decisive action that characterized the beginning of his first term. He had come into office in 1980 with a clear focus and specific goals, such as strengthening defense and cutting taxes. The 1984 election seemed to have been more about approving the job Reagan had already done, rather than encouraging ambitious new programs. As a result, when the new term began, Reagan's administration lacked the specific goals that had marked the beginning of his presidency.

In addition, the second term began with several staff changes. Jim Baker, Reagan's extremely effective chief of staff, chose to

Ronald Reagan and his vice president, George H.W. Bush, wave from the podium at the Republican National Convention in 1984. After a national economic boom and four years of charismatic leadership, Reagan was re-elected president in a landslide victory over the Democratic candidate, Walter Mondale.

switch cabinet posts with Donald Regan, the treasury secretary. Edwin Meese, the new choice for attorney general, was grilled by Congress for months before finally being approved. Reagan's close aide, Mike Deaver, also decided to leave his post and became a lobbyist. These changes meant that many of Reagan's most trusted advisers were gone.

One of the new team's initial efforts was a public relations disaster. Reagan had been invited by German Chancellor Helmut Kohl to participate in a ceremony at a German cemetery to honor the men who died in World War II. Just before the trip, it was revealed that the cemetery selected, at Bitburg, contained the bodies of 44 Nazi soldiers, including one who had received a medal for killing 10 U.S. soldiers. Both Jewish and veterans groups immediately expressed their outrage. Reagan refused to go back on his promise to Kohl, and agreed to an additional stop on his visit: the Nazi concentration camp Bergen-Belsen, where he gave a moving speech that quoted from the diary of Anne Frank.

FOREIGN POLICY

Much of Reagan's first term had focused on domestic issues—issues "at home." Cutting taxes and boosting the economy had required much of the Reagan administration's energy.

Defense policy had also played a role in the first term, and international issues would rise to center stage in Reagan's second term. In his first term of office, Reagan had increased spending to significantly boost America's military capacities. Now that he thought America was operating from a position of strength, he wanted to begin the process of negotiating with the Soviets. This task was again complicated by unresponsive Soviet leaders and by the fact that Soviet leadership changed several times while Reagan was in office.

Reagan also faced another challenge to his administration's foreign policy: terrorism. On June 14, 1985, TWA Flight 847 was hijacked shortly after takeoff from Athens,

Greece. The hijackers diverted the plane from its destination of Rome, with 153 passengers and crew members (including 135 Americans) on board, to Beirut, Lebanon. A U.S. Navy diver on the flight was brutally beaten and then shot to death, his body dumped on the airport tarmac. Some passengers and crew members were released, but 39 were held hostage in Lebanon.

It was a tricky decision; Reagan decided not to take military action, but rather to maintain his normal schedule and rely on diplomacy. By June 30, the hostages were released. This incident brought to Reagan's attention the fact that seven other Americans who were seized one at a time by kidnappers in 1984 and 1985 were still being held in Lebanon.

The hostages were believed to be held by the terrorist group Hezbollah (meaning "party of God"). Among these hostages was a CIA representative, William Buckley. The hostages were moved frequently and usually at night, so it was impossible to determine their location or mount a rescue attempt without risking civilian lives or retaliation against the hostages if the attempt failed.

Further complicating the hostage situation was its link to another foreign policy crisis point in the Middle East—the war between Iran and Iraq, which had been going on since 1980. During his first term, Reagan's foreign policy advisers had argued for U.S. support of Iraq, believing that if Iran won it would shut down much of the oil flowing out of the Persian Gulf to America. As a result, the administration's policy, launched in 1983 and called "Operation Staunch," was intended to discourage other nations from supplying Iran with weapons. This provided Iraq and its leader, Saddam Hussein, with vital assistance at a critical point in the war.

THE IRAN–CONTRA AFFAIR

By the middle of 1984, U.S. policy had left Iran desperate for weapons. In addition, the leader of Iran, Ayatollah Khomeini, was ill, possibly dying. Many potential successors were trying to position themselves to take his place.

Intelligence sources soon reported that a group of moderate Iranians would be willing to provide the United States with intelligence about the location of the hostages in Lebanon in exchange for helicopter gunships, antitank missiles, or other weapons. The president's national security adviser, Robert "Bud" McFarlane, believed that the deal would offer two pluses: an opportunity to get the hostages released and a chance to reach out to these so-called "moderate" Iranians in preparation for a time when they might be in power in Iran.

This deal would mark the beginning of a crisis that would seriously damage Ronald Reagan's presidency, a deal that became known as the Iran–Contra Affair. Reagan would later write that his focus had been on making sure that the hostages came home and that perhaps he should have listened more closely to the arguments against the deal made by some members of his cabinet. Instead, he approved the arrangements. The first weapons shipments

Robert McFarlane announces his resignation as President Reagan and John Poindexter look on in this December 4, 1985 photograph. Poindexter replaced McFarlane as national security adviser and appointed the ambitious Oliver North to oversee the Iran-Contra deal that would later bring controversy to the Reagan administration.

were delivered, but not all of the hostages were released as promised: only one was set free.

There would be many additional conversations and demands for more weapons. By December 1985, McFarlane, who had also been busy helping to arrange the Geneva meeting between Reagan and Gorbachev, was exhausted and resigned. Admiral John Poindexter became the new national security adviser. He turned over much of the day-to-day responsibility for the Iran deal to a member of his staff, Oliver North. North was a former Marine who was extremely ambitious and willing to take risks.

A new plan was created, principally at North's urging, to supply the Iranians with antitank missiles and antiaircraft missiles, with the weapons coming in small increments, one hostage being released with each shipment until all had been freed. Once again, senior members of Reagan's cabinet argued against the plan. Reagan, however, was determined to secure the release of the hostages.

When the plan again failed to obtain the release of all of the hostages, another plan was created. This time, McFarlane and North would go to Tehran, Iran, to meet directly with the so-called "moderates." The operation had the approval of CIA director William Casey, who had supplied the delegation with maps containing intelligence information on Iraq, Iran's enemy.

Given the lack of success that the operation had experienced, it is no surprise that this part was also doomed to failure. The team was ultimately forced to leave Iran without securing the release of a single hostage. Worse still, kidnappers were seizing additional hostages.

More trouble would come. Reagan's administration had initially supported the efforts of a group of rebels (Contras) in the Central American country of Nicaragua to fight against the Soviet-supported Sandinista regime that was in power. Congress had ordered a stop to any CIA or other American military or intelligence attempts to assist in the overthrow of the Nicaraguan government, but CIA director Casey continued the operation and secretly linked up with Oliver North. The two men built an entire operation supporting the Contras. They initially requested funding from countries like Saudi Arabia and Taiwan and then later gave profits left over from the Iranian arms deals (the Iranians had been vastly overcharged for weapons and spare parts) to the rebel forces.

Shortly after the midterm elections in November 1986, the story of the arms for hostages deal broke. Criticism was immediate and sweeping. Reagan initially denied the deal, and an investigation was launched.

To save his presidency and restore public confidence, Reagan fired the men who had handled the deal and replaced several members of his staff. The final step was to explain to the American people what had happened. In a nationally televised speech, he said that his belief that arms had not been traded for hostages had been proven false.

The speech restored some American confidence in Reagan's presidency, allowing him to spend the next two years focusing on negotiations with the Soviet Union. The Iran–Contra Affair, however, did not disappear with a simple speech. For the next seven years, a special prosecutor conducted a detailed investigation. The special prosecutor found that Reagan had participated in covering up the scandal but that there was no evidence that he agreed to or was aware of the diversion of money from the Iran arms sales to the Contras. In the end, most agreed that Reagan had done what he did out of a desire to bring kidnapped Americans home.

A FAILED SUMMIT FOR
NUCLEAR ARMS CONTROL

Despite the confusion created by the Iran–Contra affair, Reagan continued to press ahead with negotiation of an arms control treaty with the Soviet Union. A second summit (conference of high-level officials) to follow up on what had been achieved in Geneva was scheduled for October 11 and 12, 1986 in Reykjavik, Iceland. This meeting was more hastily arranged than the summit in Geneva had been, and the Reagan team thought that its purpose, to bring Reagan and Gorbachev back together again to map out the agenda for a third summit, would be fairly straightforward.

The team was taken by surprise when, as soon as the two leaders were seated, Gorbachev began to present a detailed plan to limit strategic weapons, intermediate-range weapons, and weapons in space. He proposed reducing strategic missiles by 50 percent and eliminating the U.S. and Soviet intermediate-range missiles based in Europe.

Reagan was not prepared for this level of discussion, nor had his team mapped out a strategy in case this type of sweeping proposal was made. On the afternoon of October 12, Gorbachev produced another stunning proposal: for both sides to do away with all nuclear weapons in 10 years.

There was one sticking point to this sweeping plan: Gorbachev insisted that Reagan's cherished plan to develop a space-based defense program (SDI, or Strategic

Reagan and Soviet leader Gorbachev left the Reykjavik, Iceland, summit grim-faced on October 12, 1986. Reagan abruptly ended the meeting, refusing to compromise his space-based defense plan in order to comply with Gorbachev's proposal that the United States and the Soviet Union eliminate their arsenals of nuclear weapons.

Defense Initiative) be confined to the research stage for the next 10 years. Reagan refused, insisting that once the technology was developed, he would share it with the Russians. He then stood up and said that the meeting was over. Gorbachev had offered to extend the summit for an additional day, but again Reagan refused. Despite the fact that some had believed that this would be a historic meeting, the two leaders left grim-faced and disappointed.

Some suggest that Reagan's refusal to give up SDI saved

the United States from potential embarrassment. A treaty to completely eliminate the Soviet and American nuclear weapons arsenals would most likely never have been approved by the Senate. The Soviet Union and its allies had an overwhelming military superiority in conventional weapons and forces. Lacking nuclear weapons, the United States would clearly be much weaker militarily. In addition, Britain and France would still have their nuclear weapons and would most likely become world powers because of them. China would also have nuclear weapons, as well as the largest standing army in the world. Rather than eliminating the threat of war, such a treaty could have made war a real possibility. Most Americans supported the president for his handling of the negotiations, believing that he had "stood tough" when he needed to.

> *"The challenge of statesmanship is to have the vision to dream of a better, safer world and the courage, persistence, and patience to turn that dream into reality."*
> — Reagan's remarks to the U.S. Negotiating Team for Nuclear & Space Arms Negotiations with the Soviet Union, March 8, 1985

The Reykjavik summit, despite ending in apparent failure, would prove to be the turning point in relations between the Soviet Union and the United States.

CHALLENGE AT BRANDENBURG

In the course of the Reykjavik meetings, both sides had come close to finalizing an agreement to eliminate medium-range missiles in Europe. This would become known as the Intermediate Nuclear Forces (INF) treaty.

It took several months of intense negotiations, but both sides finally confirmed the treaty in September 1987.

Both Reagan and Gorbachev faced domestic challenges after the summit. Reagan was dealing with the Iran–Contra affair; in the Soviet Union, Gorbachev was attempting to rescue a failing economy. Both men were also facing increasingly vocal opposition leaders.

One of the most dramatic moments of Reagan's presidency came in 1987, during a 10-day visit to Europe. On June 12, 1987, Reagan went to West Berlin and stood at the Brandenburg Gate. At the time, Europe was divided in two (with Eastern Europe allied with the Soviet Union and Western Europe allied with the United States). The city of Berlin itself was divided by a wall. The Berlin Wall was a vivid symbol of the Cold War and demonstrated with barbed wire people's inability to pass freely between East Germany and West Germany.

Even though relations between the Soviet Union and the United States were improving, Reagan showed once more that he was unwilling to negotiate from a position of weakness. In the speech, he called on Gorbachev to begin a new era:

General Secretary Gorbachev, if you seek peace, if you seek prosperity for the Soviet Union and Eastern Europe, if you seek liberalization: Come here to this gate! Mr. Gorbachev, open this gate! Mr. Gorbachev, tear down this wall!

It was one of the defining speeches of his presidency. Reagan's words echoed around the world. Less than nine months after he left office, the Berlin Wall would be torn down.

THE END OF THE EVIL EMPIRE

On December 8, 1987, the third summit between Reagan and Gorbachev began in Washington, D.C., with a historic gesture. Seated side by side, the two leaders signed

---

THE REAGAN LEGACY

The Fall of the Berlin Wall

On June 2, 1987, President Ronald Reagan stood at the Brandenburg Gate in Berlin and called on Soviet chairman Mikhail Gorbachev to tear down the wall that divided Germany—and, in effect, Europe—in two. Little more than two years later, in the fall of 1989, the Berlin Wall would be torn down.

In May 1989, Mikhail Gorbachev had visited West Germany, and he delivered a startling announcement to Chancellor Helmut Kohl: The Soviet Union would no longer use force to prevent the Soviet states in Eastern Europe from moving toward democracy. Protests spread throughout East German cities, and the tyrannical ruler of East Germany, Erich Honecker, was forced to step down. On November 9, East German officials announced that the borders were now open to the West. Within hours, Germans from both sides appeared at the wall carrying hammers and picks. The collapse of the wall quickly led to the end of the Republic of East Germany and later to the collapse of the Soviet Union.

Reagan had understood that a wall designed to keep people in rather than keep enemies out would never last. Today, the place where the Berlin Wall once divided Germany is barely visible. A stretch of about 12 miles in downtown Berlin is marked with a double line of paving stones, and a few memorials show evidence of where a city was once divided in two.

the INF Treaty, the first U.S.–Soviet accord to reduce nuclear weapons and to allow on-site monitors (representatives from the two nations to ensure compliance). On that occasion, as many times before, Reagan quoted the Soviet saying *Doverey, no proverey*: Trust but verify.

In May 1988, Reagan attended another summit, this one in Moscow. It was clear that U.S.–Soviet relations had entered a new era when the president who had once labeled the Soviet Union an "evil empire" referred to Gorbachev as "my friend."

7

THE REAGAN REVOLUTION

THE SUCCESS IN Moscow, the historic treaty, and the demonstration of American strength ensured that Reagan would finish out his presidency as popular with the American people as when he was first elected. On January 20, 1989, Reagan's vice president, George H.W. Bush, became the 41st president of the United States. The Reagan legacy lived on long after he left the Oval Office. Reagan defined his decade, shaping much of what was good or bad about the 1980s. He dramatically transformed the way Americans thought about their country and their president, instilling a sense of national pride and providing Americans with a greater sense of optimism than they had under previous leaders.

After serving faithfully as Ronald Reagan's vice president for eight years, George H.W. Bush successfully campaigned for the 1988 presidential election. Bush was sworn in as the 41st president of the United States on January 20, 1989.

Reagan was expected to accomplish great things domestically when he was first elected, and the greatest concerns expressed about his abilities were in foreign policy. Yet this area would provide him with his greatest triumphs, whereas much of his domestic policy fell short of what he had hoped to achieve.

The connection Reagan established with Gorbachev, which led to the INF treaty, was perhaps his most important legacy. It led to the end of the Cold War and, in many ways, to the end of the Soviet Union itself.

Part of Reagan's success came from his ability to portray himself as a "citizen politician," an ordinary American who had been called temporarily to service but who would never define himself as a career politician. He believed that government was a disruptive force that needed to be cut back to allow ordinary Americans to go about the business of making their country and their lives better.

Despite the so-called "sleaze factor" that involved the administration in multiple legal proceedings, an important piece of Reagan's legacy can be found in the area of the judiciary. He dramatically changed the nature of the court system, placing 3 conservative Supreme Court justices, 78 appeals court judges, and 290 district court judges (slightly more than half of the federal judiciary) during his term. He kept his campaign promise to nominate the first woman to the Supreme Court and nominated the first justice of Italian descent. These nominees generally favored judicial restraint, or avoiding over-regulating American society.

Reagan's focus on economic issues during his first term brought quick results, but they came with a price. The economy boomed during much of the 1980s, but it was pushed along by spending and debt of individuals and the government as a whole. The federal deficit grew, and this, too, is part of Reagan's legacy, the result of his never submitting a balanced budget.

Reagan had promised to create what he called a "North American accord" (an economic alliance between the North American nations) when he campaigned in 1979.

Ronald Reagan salutes his honor guard as he leaves Washington, D.C., after eight years as president. Reagan's legacy lives on long after his departure from the White House; his revitalization of the American dream, optimistic outlook, and patriotic vision of the United States as a "shining city on a hill" continue to influence the way Americans see themselves today.

After becoming president, he took steps to create free trade agreements between the United States and Canada and between the United States and Mexico.

Many of Reagan's foreign policy decisions were made for strategic reasons but resulted in problems that future presidents would be forced to resolve. When the Soviet Union invaded Afghanistan, the United States assisted the rebels fighting back. Among these rebels was a wealthy Arab named Osama bin Laden, who would establish a presence among the rebels in Afghanistan once the Soviets left and later fund the September 11, 2001 attacks against the United States.

Reagan's decision to launch an arms embargo against Iran early in the Iran–Iraq War strengthened the position of Iraq and its leader, Saddam Hussein. Future presidents would be left to deal with the legacy of these policies and the anti-Americanism of both Hussein and bin Laden.

THE GREAT COMMUNICATOR

The president who was known as the "Great Communicator" would spend his final days struggling to communicate with his friends and family. In November 1994, Reagan announced that he was suffering from Alzheimer's disease and retired to a quiet private life.

To many who lived through the Reagan years and remembered what had come before, his most important legacy was an emotional one. During Reagan's presidency, there was a sense that anything was possible. For the first time in many years, Americans felt proud of their country. The distrust sparked by the scandals of the Nixon administration and the failings of the Carter administration were replaced by belief in American ideals. Many who knew Reagan well insist that this was not politics—that the

> "The house we hope to build is not for my generation but for yours. It is your future that matters. And I hope that when you are my age, you will be able to say as I have been able to say: We lived in freedom. We lived lives that were a statement, not an apology."
>
> — Reagan's remarks to the students and faculty at St. John's University, March 28, 1985

great "shining city on a hill" he spoke of so often reflected his true belief in his country.

In his farewell address on January 11, 1989, the ever-patriotic Reagan credited American ideals, not his own talent as a politician, with shaping America's sense of destiny during the 1980s:

> I never thought it was my style or the words I used that made a difference: it was the content. I wasn't a great communicator, but I communicated great things, and they didn't spring full bloom from my brow, they came from the heart of a great nation—from our experience, our wisdom, and our belief in the principles that have guided us for two centuries. They called it the Reagan revolution. Well, I'll accept that, but for me it always seemed more like the great rediscovery, a rediscovery of our values and our common sense.

THE
PRESIDENTS
OF THE
UNITED STATES

George Washington
1789–1797

John Adams
1797–1801

Thomas Jefferson
1801–1809

James Madison
1809–1817

James Monroe
1817–1825

John Quincy Adams
1825–1829

Andrew Jackson
1829–1837

Martin Van Buren
1837–1841

William Henry
Harrison
1841

John Tyler
1841–1845

James Polk
1845–1849

Zachary Taylor
1849–1850

Millard Filmore
1850–1853

Franklin Pierce
1853–1857

James Buchanan
1857–1861

Abraham Lincoln
1861–1865

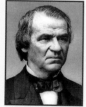
Andrew Johnson
1865–1869

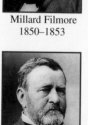
Ulysses S. Grant
1869–1877

Rutherford B. Hayes
1877–1881

James Garfield
1881

Chester Arthur
1881–1885

Grover Cleveland
1885–1889

Benjamin Harrison
1889-1893

Grover Cleveland
1893-1897

William McKinley
1897–1901

Theodore Roosevelt
1901–1909

William H. Taft
1909–1913

Woodrow Wilson
1913–1921

Warren Harding
1921–1923

Calvin Coolidge
1923–1929

Herbert Hoover
1929–1933

Franklin D. Roo-
sevelt 1933–1945

Harry S. Truman
1945–1953

Dwight Eisenhower
1953–1961

John F. Kennedy
1961–1963

Lyndon Johnson
1963–1969

Richard Nixon
1969–1974

Gerald Ford
1974–1977

Jimmy Carter
1977–1981

Ronald Reagan
1981–1989

George H.W. Bush
1989–1993

William J. Clinton
1993–2001

George W. Bush
2001–

Note: Dates indicate years of
presidential service.
Source: www.whitehouse.gov

85

PRESIDENTIAL FACT FILE

THE CONSTITUTION

Article II of the Constitution of the United States outlines several require-
ments for the president of the United States, including:

- ★ **Age:** The president must be at least 35 years old.

- ★ **Citizenship:** The president must be a U.S. citizen.

- ★ **Residency:** The president must have lived in the United States for
  at least 14 years.

- ★ **Oath of Office:** On his inauguration, the president takes this oath:
  "I do solemnly swear (or affirm) that I will faithfully execute
  the office of President of the United States, and will to the best
  of my ability, preserve, protect and defend the Constitution of
  the United States."

- ★ **Term:** A presidential term lasts four years.

PRESIDENTIAL POWERS

The president has many distinct powers as outlined in and interpreted
from the Constitution. The president:

- ★ Submits many proposals to Congress for regulatory, social, and
  economic reforms.

- ★ Appoints federal judges with the Senate's approval.

- ★ Prepares treaties with foreign nations to be approved by the
  Senate.

- ★ Can veto laws passed by Congress.

- ★ Acts as commander in chief of the military to oversee military
  strategy and actions.

- ★ Appoints members of the Cabinet and many other agencies and
  administrations with the Senate's approval.

- ★ Can declare martial law (control of local governments within
  the country) in times of national crisis.

PRESIDENTIAL FACT FILE

TRADITION

Many parts of the presidency developed out of tradition. The traditions listed below are but a few that are associated with the U.S. presidency.

- ★ After taking his oath of office, George Washington added, "So help me God." Numerous presidents since Washington have also added this phrase to their oath.

- ★ Originally, the Constitution limited the term of the presidency to four years, but did not limit the number of terms a president could serve. Presidents, following the precedent set by George Washington, traditionally served only two terms. After Franklin Roosevelt was elected to four terms, however, Congress amended the Constitution to restrict presidents to only two.

- ★ James Monroe was the first president to have his inauguration outside the Capitol. From his inauguration in 1817 to Jimmy Carter's inauguration in 1977, it was held on the east portico of the Capitol. Ronald Reagan broke from this tradition in 1981 when he was inaugurated on the west portico to face his home state, California. Since 1981, all presidential inaugurations have been held on the west portico of the Capitol.

- ★ Not all presidential traditions are serious, however. One of the more fun activities connected with the presidency began when President William Howard Taft ceremoniously threw out the first pitch of the new baseball season in 1910.  Presidents since Taft have carried on this tradition, including Woodrow Wilson, who is pictured here as he throws the first pitch of the 1916 season. In more recent years, the president has also opened the All-Star and World Series games.

PRESIDENTIAL FACT FILE

THE WHITE HOUSE

Although George Washington was involved with the planning of the White House, he never lived there. It has been, however, the official residence of every president beginning with John Adams, the second U.S. president. The building was completed approximately in 1800, although it has undergone several renovations since then. It was the first public building constructed in Washington, D.C. The White House has 132 rooms, several of which are open to the public. Private rooms include those for administration and the president's personal residence. For an online tour of the White House and other interesting facts, visit the official White House website, *http://www.whitehouse.gov.*

THE PRESIDENTIAL SEAL

A committee began planning the presidential seal in 1777. It was completed in 1782. The seal appears as an official stamp on medals, stationery, and documents, among other items. Originally, the eagle faced right toward the

arrows (a symbol of war) that it held in its talons. In 1945, President Truman had the seal altered so that the eagle's head instead faced left toward the olive branch (a symbol of peace), because he believed the president should be prepared for war but always look toward peace.

PRESIDENT REAGAN IN PROFILE

PERSONAL

Name: Ronald Wilson Reagan

Birth date: February 6, 1911

Birth place: Tampico, Illinois

Father: Jack Reagan

Mother: Nelle Wilson

Wife: Jane Wyman (divorced); Nancy Davis

Children:
Maureen, Michael (with Wyman); Patti and Ronald (with Davis)

POLITICAL

Years in office: 1981–1989

Vice president: George H.W. Bush

Political party: Republican

Nickname: The Great Communicator

Occupations before presidency:
Radio broadcaster, actor, General Electric spokesman,
California governor

Major achievements of presidency:
End of the Cold War, economic recovery, rebirth in American
patriotism, restored public faith in presidency

Presidential library:
The Ronald Reagan Presidential Library and Museum
40 Presidential Drive
Simi Valley, CA 93065
(800) 410-8354
http://www.reagan.utexas.edu

Tributes:

Ronald Reagan Federal Building (Santa Ana, CA);
Ronald Reagan Washington National Airport (Washington, D.C.)

1911   Ronald Wilson Reagan is born in Tampico, Illinois.

1928   Reagan enrolls at Eureka College in Illinois.

1932   Reagan begins radio broadcasting career at WOC in Iowa.

1937   Reagan is offered a contract by Warner Brothers and moves to California to begin a film career.

1940   Reagan marries actress Jane Wyman.

1942   Reagan is called to active duty in Army Air Force. He is assigned to the Motion Picture Unit based in California to make military training films.

1945   Reagan is discharged from the army and resumes his acting career.

1949   Reagan and his first wife divorce.

1952   Reagan becomes the spokesman for General Electric Company. He marries Nancy Davis.

1964   Reagan gives a televised speech in support of presidential candidate Barry Goldwater. He is soon approached to run for governor of California.

1966   Reagan is elected governor of California.

1970   Reagan wins re-election as governor.

1975   Reagan becomes a presidential candidate but loses the Republican Party nomination to Gerald Ford.

1980   Reagan is elected 40th president of the United States.

1981   John Hinckley Jr. attempts to assassinate Reagan. Reagan fires air traffic controllers during their strike.

1982   The recession slows, and economic expansion begins.

1984   Reagan wins re-election in a landslide victory over Walter Mondale.

1985   Reagan meets with Soviet leader Mikhail Gorbachev in Geneva, Switzerland. His administration begins efforts to secure release of hostages held in Lebanon in operation that will become known as the Iran–Contra Affair.

1986 The second summit between Reagan and Gorbachev, held in Iceland, ends in disappointment.

1987 Reagan and Gorbachev meet in Washington and sign the INF Treaty.

1988 Reagan travels to Moscow.

1989 George H.W. Bush, vice president under Reagan, is elected president.

1994 Reagan announces that he suffers from Alzheimer's disease.

Boyarsky, Bill. *Ronald Reagan: His Life and Rise to the Presidency*. New York: Random House, 1981.

Cannon, Lou. *President Reagan: The Role of a Lifetime*. New York: Simon & Schuster, 1991.

Cannon, Lou. *Ronald Reagan: The Presidential Portfolio*. New York: Public Affairs, 2001.

Evans, Rowland, and Robert Novak. *The Reagan Revolution*. New York: E.P. Dutton, 1981.

Fitzgerald, Frances. *Way Out There in the Blue: Reagan, Star Wars and the End of the Cold War*. New York: Simon & Schuster, 2000.

Mandelbaum, Michael, and Strobe Talbott. *Reagan and Gorbachev*. New York: Vintage Books, 1987.

Mayer, Jane, and Doyle McManus. *Landslide: The Unmaking of the President, 1984–1988*. Boston: Houghton Mifflin Company, 1988.

Noonan, Peggy. *When Character was King: A Story of Ronald Reagan*. New York: Penguin Books, 2001.

Pemberton, William E. *Exit with Honor: The Life and Presidency of Ronald Reagan*. Armonk, N.Y.: M.E. Sharpe, 1997.

Reagan, Nancy. *My Turn*. New York: Random House, 1989.

Reagan, Ronald. *An American Life*. New York: Simon & Schuster, 1990.

Reagan, Ronald. *Speaking My Mind: Selected Speeches*. New York: Simon & Schuster, 1989.

Schieffer, Bob, and Gary Paul Gates. *The Acting President*. New York: E.P. Dutton, 1989.

Schweizer, Peter. *Victory: The Reagan Administration's Secret Strategy that Hastened the Collapse of the Soviet Union*. Boston: The Atlantic Monthly Press, 1994.

BIBLIOGRAPHY

WEBSITES

The American Experience: The Presidents
   www.pbs.org/wgbh/amex/presidents/

Official Website of the Ronald Reagan Presidential Library
   www.reagan.utexas.edu

The White House: The Presidents of the United States
   www.whitehouse.gov/history/presidents/

FURTHER READING

Cannon, Lou. *Ronald Reagan: The Presidential Portfolio.* New York: Public Affairs, 2001.

Noonan, Peggy. *When Character Was King: A Story of Ronald Reagan.* New York: Penguin Books, 2001.

Reagan, Ronald. *An American Life.* New York: Simon & Schuster, 1990.

Reagan, Ronald. *Speaking My Mind: Selected Speeches.* New York: Simon & Schuster, 1989.

WEBSITES

The American Presidency
www.grolier.com/presidents/

Presidents of the United States
www.ipl.org/div/potus/rwreagan.html

The American Experience: The Presidents
www.pbs.org/wgbh/amex/presidents/

The Reagan Information Exchange
www.reagan.com

Official Website of the Ronald Reagan Presidential Library
www.reagan.utexas.edu

Ronald Reagan: Official Presidential Website
www.reaganfoundation.org

Ronald Reagan Presidential Library and Museum
www.reaganlibrary.net

The White House: The Presidents of the United States
www.whitehouse.gov/history/presidents/

INDEX

INDEX

INDEX

INDEX

Picture Credits

page:

11: © Associated Press, AP

15: © Roger Ressmeyer/CORBIS

18: © Alain Nogues/CORBIS SYGMA

23: Courtesy of the National Archives

29: © Hulton|Archive, by Getty Images

32: Courtesy of the National Archives

35: © Hulton|Archive, by Getty Images

38: Courtesy of the Library of Congress
LC-USZ62-79809

41: Courtesy of the National Archives

45: © Associated Press, AP

49: © Bettmann/CORBIS

55: Courtesy of the Library of Congress/
American Memory, LC-USZC4-7727

58: Courtesy of the National Archives

61: © Associated Press, AP

65: © Peter Turnley/CORBIS

69: © Bettmann/CORBIS

73: © Associated Press, AP

79: Courtesy of the Library of Congress/
American Memory, LC-USZC4-7722

81: © CORBIS

Cover: Courtesy of the National Archives

Acknowledgments

Thank you to Celebrity Speakers Intl. for coordinating Mr. Cronkite's contribution to this book.

Heather Lehr Wagner is a writer and editor. She earned an M.A. in government from the College of William and Mary and a B.A. in political science from Duke University. She has written several books for teens on social and political issues and is also the author of *George Washington, John Adams,* and *Thomas Jefferson* in the GREAT AMERICAN PRESIDENTS series.

Walter Cronkite has covered virtually every major news event during his more than 60 years in journalism, during which he earned a reputation for being "the most trusted man in America." He began his career as a reporter for the United Press during World War II, taking part in the beachhead assaults of Normandy and covering the Nuremberg trials. He then joined *CBS News* in Washington, D.C., where he was the news anchor for political convention and election coverage from 1952 to 1980. CBS debuted its first half-hour weeknight news program with Mr. Cronkite's interview of President John F. Kennedy in 1963. Mr. Cronkite was inducted into the Academy of Television Arts and Sciences in 1985 and has written several books. He lives in New York City with his wife of 59 years.

21.85

DATE			